Polymer Clay
Jewellery Projects

Step-by-step instructions to create a collection of beautiful wearable Polymer Clay jewellery pieces

This is the book that I could never find!

How many times have you looked through a craft book to see instructions for the main feature bead or pendant and there's no information on how to make the finished design?

Using simple step by step pictures and instructions I will cover many elements of jewellery making, to help you create wonderful pieces, made entirely by you.

In the pages that follow, I'll teach you all about them.

Bulford, Debbie
Polymer Clay Jewellery Projects: Step-by-step instructions to create a collection of beautiful wearable Polymer Clay jewellery pieces

Debbie Portrait by Sally-Ann Salmon: Future Publishing
Photography by Chris Ham: www.chrishamphotography.co.uk
Edited by Sally Stevens: www.sallystevens.com
Typesetting and Design by Julie Arnett: julie.arnett@ymail.com

Published by Debbie Bulford: www.sodebbiebulford.com email: debbiebulford@aol.com

First Edition: 2013

Trademarks/Copyright details:
Premo! Sculpey Clay
Jewellery Maker TV
Lisa Pavelka

Printed and bound in the UK by Ashford Colour Press: www.ashfordcolourpress.co.uk

ISBN: 978-0-9926262-0-4

Acknowledgments

I cannot express how lucky I feel to have the support of a loving family. Thank you to my Mum and Dad for always believing in me, no matter how much mess I made! A big hug to my two wonderful boys and, last but not least, to my soul mate Bryan. Thank you for all the laughter, fun and never ending support of my dream.

It's true; sometimes you do have to be in the right place at the right time. My Mum took a selection of my jewellery to show her hairdresser, who also happened to be a hairdresser to Linda Brumwell. Linda is a member of the family-run The Genuine Gemstone Company and, when she saw my jewellery, Linda invited me to become a Guest Designer on Jewellery Maker TV. Thank you Linda for asking me to join the mad house, I love every minute!

Lastly, thank you to everyone who has attended my workshops. I never stop learning. You inspire me more than you realise.

Contents

Contents

Foreword by
Steve Bennett

Steve is the Chief Executive of the family-owned The Genuine Gemstone Company - voted the Fastest Growing Company in the UK in 2012. The passion Steve has for his trade is infectious, he is a gemstone expert, an author, and it's no surprise that the company is now the largest supplier of gemstones in the world, which encompasses four TV Channels: Gems TV, Rocks TV, Gem Collector and Jewellery Maker TV.

Debbie joined Jewellery Maker TV as a Guest Designer in 2010. Her love for colour and design is evident with every jewellery creation; it never ceases to amaze me the endless ways you can embellish and enhance genuine gemstones.

It's obvious that Debbie loves to teach, this comes across in her workshops with customers returning time after time. Her first love is Polymer Clay, the appeal spans any age: children love to be involved as much as Mums, Dads and Grandparents!

Jewellery Maker TV strives to provide our viewers with the best possible range of products to encourage their creativity and our Guest Designers are essential to achieve that goal. Products including Silver Clay, Resin, Jewel Enamel and Chain Maille are just a few of the crafts available and the list grows daily. We like to make our customers feel they are part of the Jewellery Maker experience by demonstrating as many techniques as possible, and this takes us to the next stage for Debbie, to take the plunge and put her knowledge into print. This 'project' book is perfect for both the beginner and experienced jewellery maker; it covers Polymer Clay and much more!

I know you will enjoy this book: look, learn, be creative and enjoy your Polymer Clay journey.

Best wishes,

Steve Bennett

Introduction

I am a great believer in fate!

A few years ago my love of colour and texture took me down the route of Interior Design, I was teaching Soft Furnishings at a local college but sadly a large percentage of leisure courses were cancelled and I found myself looking for another way to use my love of design.

An advert for a craft exhibition jumped out at me! I can remember watching a demonstration of Polymer Clay by Birdy Heywood, fascinated by the colours and creative possibilities with this medium.

Since that time, I've developed a range of skills and techniques. Now, I work happily with wire, polymer clay, resin, foils, fabrics and natural materials, bringing them together to make finished pieces of jewellery which please me and others too!

I am lucky to be a Guest Designer on Jewellery Maker TV, those of you who watch the show will know I have one saying 'your jewellery should be handmade not homemade', the finishing touches to your designs can make all the difference.

Now, I'm writing my first book to show you how to make a series of individual pieces from start to finish.

Let's get creative, enjoy!

Why Polymer Clay?

I have chosen Premo! Sculpey Polymer Clay for all the projects in this book. It's the only polymer clay I've found that allows you to move between black and white without having to wash your hands: as a teacher I have found that to be so important.

Polymer clay is a man made, non-toxic craft material made of tiny particles of PVC (poly vinyl chloride), pigment and a plasticizer. Each brand has a slightly different characteristic, finish and baking temperature, so always check the manufacturer's instructions on the packaging before you begin.

Working with Polymer Clay:

✔ Always 'condition' or soften your clay before use. Slice your clay and roll each slice by hand into a log of clay then roll with an acrylic roller or use your clay roller. Try not to overwork your clay, it can become too soft. When you have made a cane, place it in the fridge for an hour to return it to its original firm consistency, this will stop the canes distorting when you slice them.

✔ Keep your unused polymer clay colours and scrap clay in storage boxes with the number 5 on the base. If you use clear flimsy food storage boxes the clay will melt into the plastic. Or, store your unbaked beads and canes wrapped in parchment paper. I have canes that are five years old and I still use them in projects today.

Polymer Clay Baking Tips:

✔ Polymer clay is simple, quick and easy to bake. Premo! Sculpey Polymer Clay bakes at 275 °F (130 °C) for between 15-30 minutes depending on the thickness of your design. The colours of clay will fuse together in the oven but will only harden as it cools, this takes approximately twenty minutes. If your design is still soft you will need to bake it again. It is recommended to bake your creation 20 mins for every ¼ inch (6mm) thickness.

✔ Polymer clay can easily be baked in your home oven, or you can use a small camping oven. A timer is an essential. If the phone rings, someone arrives at your door, or you are busy making some new designs, it is so easy to forget the time!

✔ You can bake your clay as many times as you like without damaging it.

Safety precautions:

Clay rollers and pasta rollers are one and the same. But never use food in a pasta roller once it has been used for clay rolling.

A microwave oven is not suitable for baking polymer clay.

Always follow the manufacturer's instructions when baking your clay. Bake your clay in a covered container (an old baking tin covered with foil is perfect).
Do not bake polymer clay alongside food.

If you burn the clay, switch off the oven and ventilate the room. The fumes are not toxic but the smell is unpleasant.

The Polymer Clay community is generous and friendly and always open to sharing techniques. The British Polymer Clay Guild is a fabulous group of like-minded people; their website has a wealth of talent, inspiration and information.
Visit www.bpcg.org.uk for more information.

Have fun with your polymer clay creations. It's easy to use and there is no waste, so don't be afraid to have a go!

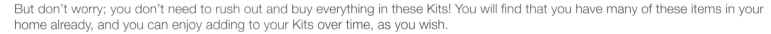

How to use this book!

I have included a wide variety of Polymer Clay and Jewellery Making techniques in this book. So, rather than repeat lists of clay tools, embellishments and jewellery findings with each project, the following pages suggest a selection of useful 'Kits' that will be helpful for your creative journey.

But don't worry; you don't need to rush out and buy everything in these Kits! You will find that you have many of these items in your home already, and you can enjoy adding to your Kits over time, as you wish.

Polymer Clay:

First Steps Kit:
tools to cut and smooth your clay

Surface Design Kit:
materials to give your clay shape and texture

Embellishing Kit:
add sparkle and glamour to your clay with foils, Mica powder and more!

Finishing Kit:
tools for baking, sanding and varnishing your clay

Jewellery Making:

Tool Kit:
basic tools for making your jewellery

Threading Kit:
essential threading materials to complete jewellery designs

Findings Kit:
all of the findings used in this book

Polymer Clay First Steps Kit:

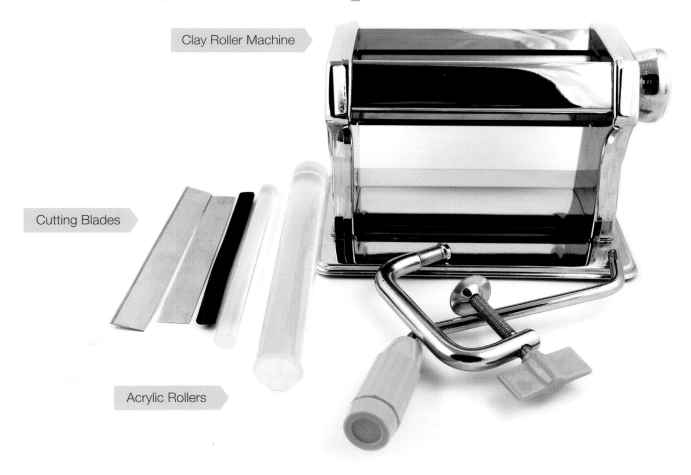

Clay Roller Machine

Cutting Blades

Acrylic Rollers

Cutting Blades: known as 'tissue' blades, these very sharp blades can be firm or flexible, straight or serrated, and are usually supplied with a rubber safety guard

Acrylic Rollers: both flat and round, to flatten sheets of clay for bangles and roll logs of clay for tubes

Clay Roller Machine : an invaluable piece of equipment to help you condition your clay quickly and easily and to give you 'uniform' sheets of clay. Usually supplied with a handle and a clamp to attach to a table.

Polymer Clay
Surface Design:

Extruder

Texture Sheets

Cable Needle

Moulds

Clay Cutters

Moulds:	an optional extra to your design collection. Can be used to create feature pieces and to give a perfect replica of an existing piece of jewellery for each bead or pendant.
Texture Sheets:	an optional extra to your design collection. Can be used to give texture and design to your creations.
Extruder:	used to extrude clay in tubes of various shapes.
Cable Needle:	can be used as a rolling pin, or to smooth seams on beads and pendants.
Clay Cutters :	a selection of catering and craft cutters to cut various shapes and sizes from clay.

Polymer Clay
Embellishing:

Liquid Clay

Gem Art

Metallic Powders

Metallic Flakes

Acrylic Paint

Lisa Pavelka Foils

Gleam

Lisa Pavelka Foils:	these foils give a beautiful high gloss metallic finish to your clay.
Gem Art:	an optional extra to your design collection. Tiny particles of genuine gemstones to add texture and value to your designs. Gem Art is available from The Genuine Gemstone Company Ltd: www.jewellerymaker.com
Liquid Clay:	used to bond baked and unbaked clay together. Can be tinted or used as a varnish.
Metallic Powders:	can be applied with a brush or your finger tip, to highlight texture and create decorative finishes.
Acrylic Paint:	an optional extra to your design collection. Can be used to create an aged effect or a patina on the clay.
Metallic Flakes:	these give a metallic finish to your clay designs.
Gleam:	a wax-based pigment, which can be applied to baked clay and various other surfaces. Leave to dry then buff to a sheen.

Polymer Clay Finishing Kit:

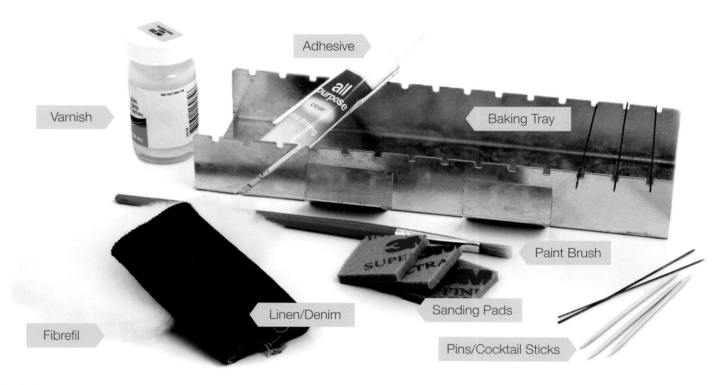

Adhesive

Varnish

Baking Tray

Paint Brush

Linen/Denim

Sanding Pads

Fibrefil

Pins/Cocktail Sticks

Varnish:	only for use on baked clay. Always use water based varnish such as manufacturers' 'own' brands. Solvent-based varnish will not dry on Polymer Clay.
Adhesive:	use jewellery glue or clear nail varnish to seal knots or to secure a bail to a pendant.
Baking Tray:	a purpose-made baking tray for pendants and beads. You can also use a metal food tray.
Fibrefil:	useful to stop any pressure marks on the clay, whilst baking your designs.
Linen/Denim :	used as polishing cloths to buff your finished designs.
Paint Brush:	to apply varnish.
Sanding Pads:	you will need 'wet and dry' pads: 400, 600 and 800 grit sanding pads are suitable to smooth your baked clay designs. The pads must always be used wet, on clay submersed in water, to avoid scratching.
Pins/Cocktail Sticks:	used to make holes in beads and pendants.
Heatproof tile:	used for baking flat pieces of jewellery. Household tiles can be used.

Beading Tools:

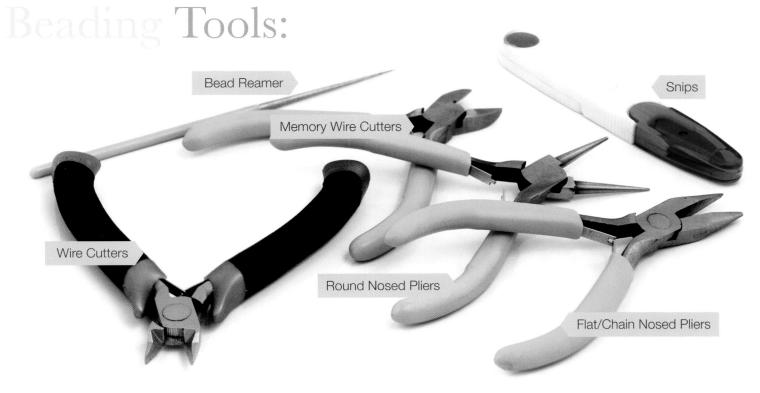

Bead Reamer

Snips

Memory Wire Cutters

Wire Cutters

Round Nosed Pliers

Flat/Chain Nosed Pliers

Gizmo

Bead Reamer:	a sharp file, used to make the holes in your beads larger.
Snips:	for snipping thread and elastic.
Memory Wire Cutters:	extra strong pliers for cutting memory wire.
Wire Cutters:	useful to stop any pressure marks on the clay, whilst baking your designs.
Round Nosed Pliers:	used for creating loops and curves in wire.
Flat/Chain Nosed Pliers:	for squashing crimp beads, holding, bending and straightening wire.
Gizmo:	a coiling gadget with two mandrels used to produce wire coils and jump rings. You can attach your Gizmo to a small piece of wood, to protect your work surface and to make it easier to hold.

Beading Threading Kit:

Beading Wire

Beading Elastic

Monofilament

Chain

Memory Wire

Cord

Beading Thread:	nylon-coated stainless steel strands for your beading projects.
Beading Elastic:	coloured and transparent elastic, perfect for simple bracelets and for people who have an allergy to metal findings.
Monofilament:	transparent nylon beading thread, an alternative thread for stringing beads, bracelets and illusion necklaces.
Cord:	nylon and silk for stringing pearls, leather and cotton cord for macramé and necklace strings.
Beading Wire:	available in a variety of gauges. An addition to your jewellery designs, ideal for making bails for polymer clay pendants and can be baked in the oven.
Chain:	can be baked with the clay, in your oven, perfect to hang your jewellery designs from.
Memory Wire:	pre-formed wire which has a memory and will keep its original shape. Available in ring, bracelet and necklace forms.

Beading Findings Kit:

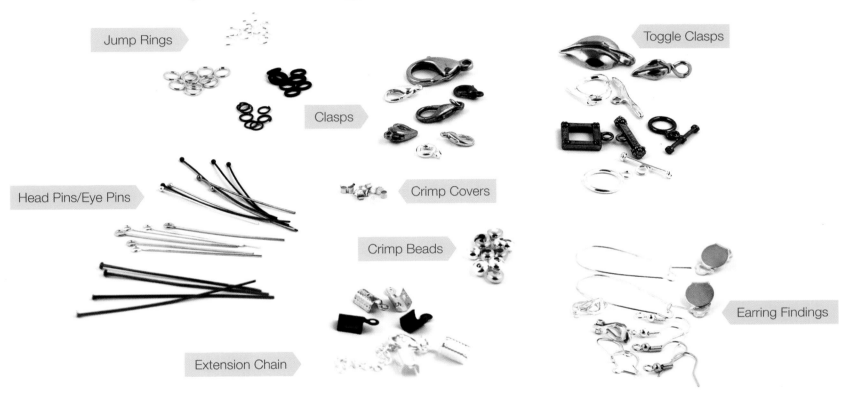

Jump Rings

Toggle Clasps

Clasps

Head Pins/Eye Pins

Crimp Covers

Crimp Beads

Earring Findings

Extension Chain

Head Pins/Eye Pins : a head pin can have a ball or a 'T' head at one end. An eye pin has a loop at one end.

Jump Rings: split, open and closed jump rings.

Crimp Beads: for securing your clasp and can be used as spacer beads.

Crimp Covers: used to cover and neaten your crimp beads.

Extension Chain: to extend the length of your designs.

Clasps: bolt ring and lobster claw clasps. Used to secure your jewellery pieces.

Toggle Clasp: a two-part clasp with a loop and a bar. Used to secure jewellery pieces.

Earring Findings: shepherd hook and clip earrings.

Colours of
the Rainbow

There are times when I finish a project and take a look at the left over clay, and realise that the colour combinations are just too beautiful to throw on the scrap clay pile.

It's a wonderful surprise when you spend time putting together a colour combination for a project, only to find that the scrap clay leftovers look even better!

So let's use them!

Onion Bead Necklace

Combine Polymer Clay with bold feature beads to create a contemporary piece of jewellery.

Ingredients

- ☑ Polymer clay: half a block each of Antique Gold, Black, White and Silver
- ☑ Scrap clay
- ☑ 32 Haematite faceted rondelles 8mm x 5mm
- ☑ Two Black cage beads 30cm of 5mm rubber tubing
- ☑ Ruler

Instructions To make 'new clay' beads:

1 Condition each of the four clay colours. Roll each one through your clay roller on setting number 1.

2 Stack the clays on top of each other, it doesn't matter which order you choose. Roll the clay into a log and twist it. Fold the log in half and twist again. Roll the log through your clay roller on setting number 3, to produce a striped sheet.

3 Hand roll a log of scrap clay, approximately 1cm in diameter, for the inside of the beads. Slice into three 2cm long tubes.

To make 'scrap clay' beads:

4 Cut the striped clay into three rectangles, each approximately 3cm x 4cm. Place a scrap clay tube in the centre of each one.

5 Wrap a rectangle of striped clay around each tube. Roll each one in the palm of your hand to make a round bead. Make a hole in each bead large enough to thread the rubber cording through. Bake the clay beads according to the manufacturer's instructions.

Roll scrap clay into a log and twist it. Fold the log in half and twist again. Hand roll a log of scrap clay, approximately 1.5cm in diameter, for the inside of the beads. Slice into three 2cm long tubes. Roll each one in the palm of your hand to make a round bead. Make a hole in each bead large enough to feed the rubber cording through. Bake the clay beads according to the manufacturer's instructions.

Making up the design:

1 Thread eight haematite beads onto a short length of beading thread and tie the ends in a secure knot, forming a ring of beads.

2 Weave the ends of the thread back through the adjacent beads and trim. Repeat to make four identical rings of haematite beads.

3 Cut a length of beading thread about 20cm longer than you require for your necklace. Thread a crimp and a jump ring onto one end. Take the end of the thread back through the crimp. Push the crimp up to the jump ring, and squash the crimp firmly with flat nosed pliers. Trim excess beading thread close to the crimp.

4 Cut rubber tubing to the length required for your necklace. Thread the beading thread through the tubing and push the tubing up to the crimp bead. Thread your onion beads, haematite bead rings and cage beads onto the tubing as shown.

5 Thread a crimp and a clasp onto the other end of the beading thread as in Step 9. Take the end of the thread back through the crimp and pull it firmly to secure the clasp close to the end of the tubing. Squash the crimp firmly with flat nosed pliers. Trim excess beading thread close to the crimp.

6 Secure crimp covers over your crimp beads to finish.

Crescent Bead Necklace

Softly curved beads fit together to give texture
and interest to the finished design.

Ingredients

- ☑ Polymer clay: half a block each of Pearl, Black, White and Silver
- ☑ Scrap clay
- ☑ Beading thread
- ☑ 40 Haematite tubes 7mm x 5mm
- ☑ Ruler
- ☑ Knitting needle
- ☑ Acrylic rolling sheet

Instructions To make 'new clay' beads:

1 Condition each of the four clay colours. Roll each one through your clay roller on setting number 1. Stack the clays on top of each other, roll into a log and twist. Use an acrylic rolling sheet to smooth into a long tube about 5mm to 7mm in diameter.

2 Placing a ruler alongside the tube for guidance, slice the clay into approximately thirty 2cm long tubes.

3 Roll your finger over each end of a tube to form a large rice-shaped bead. Repeat for all thirty beads.

To make 'scrap clay' beads:

4 Bend each bead over a knitting needle to form a crescent. Make a hole in each bead with a pin or a cocktail stick. Bake the clay beads according to the manufacturer's instructions.

Roll scrap clay into a log and twist it. Use an acrylic sheet to smooth into a long tube about 5mm to 7mm in diameter. Placing a ruler alongside the tube for guidance, slice the clay into thirty 2cm long tubes. Roll your finger over each end of a tube to form a large rice-shaped bead. Repeat for all thirty beads. Bend each bead over a knitting needle to form a crescent. Make a hole in each bead with a pin or a cocktail stick. Bake the clay beads according to the manufacturer's instructions.

Making up the design:

1 Cut a length of beading thread about 20cm longer than you require for your necklace. Thread a crimp and a jump ring onto one end. Take the end of the thread back through the crimp. Push the crimp up to the jump ring, and squash the crimp firmly with flat nosed pliers. Trim excess beading thread close to the crimp.

2 Thread 15 haematite tubes onto the beading thread. Thread on a pair of crescent beads, facing each other, then one haematite tube, repeat until you have used all of the crescent beads. Thread on 15 haematite tubes to match the first side of your necklace.

3 Thread a crimp and a clasp onto the other end of the beading thread as in Step 1. Take the end of the thread back through the crimp and pull it firmly to secure the clasp close to the last Haematite bead. Squash the crimp firmly with flat nosed pliers. Trim excess beading thread close to the crimp.

Multi Strand
Tube Necklace

This necklace would be perfect for a summer's
evening to combine with a cool fresh linen outfit.

Ingredients

- ☑ Polymer clay: half a block each of Turquoise, Translucent and Pearl
- ☑ 50 Pyrite rondelles 8mm x 3mm
- ☑ 12 Pyrite rondelles 5mm x 3mm
- ☑ Ruler
- ☑ Acrylic rolling sheet

Instructions

Making up the design:

1 Condition each of the three clay colours. Divide the translucent clay into two equal pieces. Add a pea-sized pinch of turquoise clay to half a block of translucent clay. Mix together by rolling in your hands at first, then pass through your clay roller several times on a medium setting, usually number 4 or 5, until the mix is a uniform shade. Roll the mixed clay into a log. Roll each of the remaining Translucent, Turquoise and Pearl clays into separate logs.

2 Use an acrylic rolling sheet to smooth each of the four logs into a long tube about 5mm in diameter. Placing a ruler alongside the tubes for guidance, slice the clays into approximately 40 tubes, each 1.5cm long. Make a hole in each bead with a pin or a cocktail stick. Ensure the hole is large enough to pass your beading thread through. Use the acrylic rolling sheet to smooth the surface again, if necessary. Bake the clay beads according to the manufacturer's instructions.

1 Cut three lengths of beading thread about 20cm longer than you require for your necklace. Make up as three separate necklaces: thread a crimp and a jump ring onto one end of the thread. Take the end of the thread back through the crimp. Push the crimp up to the jump ring, and squash the crimp firmly with flat nosed pliers. Trim excess beading thread close to the crimp. Repeat for each length. Add crimp covers to finish each strand.

2 On each strand, thread two small and one large Pyrite rondelle. Select the clay tubes at random and follow the pattern of: one tube, one rondelle, one tube, until you have 11 tubes on the centre strand, 12 tubes on the middle strand and 13 tubes on the outer strand.

3 Then add one large and two small Pyrite rondelles on the other end of each strand and complete with a crimp, a jump ring and a crimp cover.

4 To finish, secure the three strands together with a large jump ring at each end. Attach a clasp to one end and a second large jump ring at the other.

Simple one strand
tube necklace with
Haematite tubes.

Add wire, coiled
with a Gizmo, and
various shapes
and sizes of beads
to change the look
of your design.

Curved Disc Bracelet

The curves of this Polymer Clay bracelet sit beautifully together on the wrist.

Ingredients

- ☑ Polymer clay: half a block each of White Granite and Grey Granite
- ☑ 108 Haematite rondelles 5mm x 1mm
- ☑ Beading elastic
- ☑ Circular clay cutter 12mm

Instructions

1 Roll both clay colours through your clay roller on the thickest setting, usually number 1. Cut nine discs of each colour, using a 12mm diameter round clay cutter. You may need to experiment at first to find the right size of disc to curve around your Haematite rondelles. Place the clay discs over a knitting needle to form a curve as in the picture. Make two holes in each side of every curved disc, with a pin or a cocktail stick. Ensure the holes are large enough to pass the beading elastic through. Place the curved discs onto a heatproof tile that will fit into your oven. Bake the discs according to the manufacturer's instructions.

2 Cut two lengths of beading elastic, about 20cm longer than you require for your bracelet. Thread one length of elastic through the top hole in each disc, securing three Haematite rondelles inside each curve. Repeat for the second hole in each disc. Tie the ends of the elastic together to finish and add a drop of jewellery glue or clear nail varnish to secure.

It's as easy as that!

Make a disc necklace: cut flat discs of polymer clay, graduating in size, and make a hole in the centre of each one with a pin or a cocktail stick before baking, to make a really simple but effective necklace.

Make discs whenever you have beautiful scrap clay. Put them aside until you have enough to make another bracelet or necklace.

There will never be any waste with this hobby!

Adding Sparkle & Shine

There are many ways to add a little extra glamour to your jewellery designs.

Foils are metallic coatings supplied on plastic sheets, and which can be transferred to clay and other surfaces using gentle pressure or heat.

Metallic leaf is sold in packs of very thin sheets or flakes and it sticks to clay instantly.

Mica powders are very exciting; they give an instant lift to a simple design and are perfect for highlighting textures and designs, or to give a vintage feel to your jewellery creations. The powders need to be sealed after application so that they don't rub off with wear.

Squiggle Necklace

The simple but effective technique gives texture
and drama to this necklace.

Ingredients

- ☑ Polymer Clay: One block of Black, a quarter block of Olive
- ☑ Zesty Lime Mica Powder
- ☑ Peridot Gem Art
- ☑ Four 1cm x 7mm and four 7mm x 3mm Black Onyx rondelles
- ☑ Eight 5mm, fourteen 7mm and four 11mm Forest Green Faceted Shell Pearls
- ☑ Extruder tool (optional)
- ☑ Ruler
- ☑ PVA glue

Instructions

1 Condition the Black clay. Roll it through your clay roller on the thickest setting, usually number 1. Roll the entire block into a 1.5cm diameter tube. Placing a ruler alongside the tube for guidance, slice off a 4cm length.

2 Roll the remaining Black clay to reduce it to a 1cm diameter tube. Slice off two 3cm lengths. From the remainder, pinch off sufficient Black clay to roll out two identical rice-shaped beads approximately 5mm wide and 1.5cm long.

3 Push the left over Black clay into an extruder fitted with a single hole disc. Extrude a long fine string of clay. Randomly drape the string over each bead to give a 'squiggle' effect.

4 Mica powders can dramatically change the look of clay. I have used a beautiful Zesty Lime which, when added to the black, takes on the look of gunmetal. Dip your finger into the powder and rub it gently onto your clay beads.

5 Condition the Olive clay. Roll it through your clay roller on the thickest setting, usually number 1. Make two beads approximately 1cm round. Make a hole in each bead with a pin or a cocktail stick. Coat the beads in PVA glue and then roll them in the Gem Art. Bake all of the clay beads according to the manufacturer's instructions.

Making up the design:

1 Cut a length of beading thread about 20cm longer than you require for your choker. Thread a crimp and a jump ring onto one end. Take the end of the thread back through the crimp. Push the crimp up to the jump ring, and squash the crimp firmly with flat nosed pliers. Trim excess beading thread close to the crimp.

2 On a beading mat or tray, lay out the rondelle and pearl beads to build your design. Thread them onto your beading thread. Thread a crimp and a clasp onto the other end of the beading thread as in Step 1. Take the end of the thread back through the crimp and pull it firmly to secure the clasp close to the last bead. Squash the crimp firmly.

A squiggle feature bead with a stunning tassel.

This technique can also be used to create beautifully textured rings.

Layered Pendant

Mix and match shapes and textures to create
your own unique layered design.

Ingredients

- ☑ Polymer clay: half a block of Black and a quarter block of Old Gold
- ☑ Gold Mica powder
- ☑ Lisa Pavelka texture sheet of your choice
- ☑ 1/2m of 5mm black rubber tubing
- ☑ 30cm of 0.8mm gauge Antique bronze wire
- ☑ Beading thread
- ☑ 1cm, 3cm and 4cm diameter circular clay cutters
- ☑ Feature design clay cutter

Instructions

1 Condition the Black clay. Roll it through your clay roller on the thickest setting, usually number 1. Using your clay cutters, cut out a 4cm circle and the feature design.

2 Fold the remaining Black clay in half to create a double thickness. Press your texture sheet firmly into the clay.

3 Gently rub gold Mica powder over the textured pattern. Next, rub Mica powder over the cut out feature design.

4 Use the 4cm cutter to cut out a textured pattern circle. Build your design by placing the 3cm black clay circle on top of the patterned circle. Add the feature design to the centre of the pendant.

5 Cut out a 1cm circle at the top for suspending the pendant. Bake the clay pendant according to the manufacturer's instructions.

6 Cut a 10cm length of rubber tubing. Cut a 30cm length of Antique bronze wire. Coil one end of the wire six times around one prong of your round nosed pliers and thread the other end through the 10cm length of tubing. Create a matching coil at the other end of the wire.

7 Cut a 15cm length of Antique bronze wire. Thread one end of the wire through the pendant and twist it around the other end to secure the wire at the top of the pendant as shown. Trim off the excess wire.

8 Form a curve in the wire using your round nosed pliers and place it over the centre of the shorter length piece of rubber tubing. Continue to curl the wire over the shorter length of tubing, forming a double coil. Cut a 45cm length of rubber tubing to make a choker length necklace. Thread the ends of the choker length tubing through the coils of wire at each end of the shorter length of tubing.

9 Cut a length of beading thread about 20cm longer than you require for your choker. Thread a crimp and a jump ring onto one end. Take the end of the thread back through the crimp. Push the crimp up to the jump ring, and squash the crimp firmly with flat nosed pliers. Trim excess beading thread close to the crimp. Pass the beading thread through the choker length of tubing.

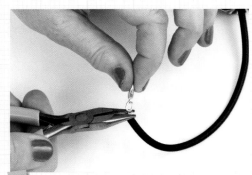

10 Thread a crimp and a clasp onto the other end of the beading thread as in Step 9. Take the end of the thread back through the crimp and pull it firmly to secure the clasp close to the tubing. Squash the crimp firmly with flat nosed pliers. Trim excess beading thread close to the crimp.

Hollow Pendant

I first saw Debbie Carlton create this pendant, I love the perfect curves and the 'light as a feather' feel.

Ingredients

- ☑ Polymer clay: one block of Bronze
- ☑ Scrap clay (optional)
- ☑ Copper/gold foil flakes
- ☑ Two 2cm decorative copper beads
- ☑ One 3cm wooden hollow disc bead
- ☑ 1m of 1.5mm cotton cord
- ☑ 1m of 0.8 gauge copper wire
- ☑ 5cm and 1.5cm circular clay cutters
- ☑ Gizmo Wire Coiling Tool

Instructions

1 Condition the clay. Roll it through your clay roller on the thickest setting, usually number 1. Cut the clay in half. Sprinkle a little of the foil flakes on top of the first piece of clay, pushing the flakes into the clay. Do not rub, or the flakes will just become a pile of glittery dust! Continue until the surface is covered.

2 Place the clay, foil side down, on top of the cutting edge of the larger circular cutter. Press down with your fingers to form a dip in the clay.

3 Quickly flip over the cutter and place the clay 'dome' onto the second piece of clay.

4 Press the smaller round cutter into the clay.

5 Remember! When you lift this pendant it is easy to squash the 'dome', so use one of your tissue blades to lift the pendant.

6 Push a pin down through the top of the pendant. Bake the clay pendant according to the manufacturer's instructions.

7 Pass 10cm of wire through one side of the wooden disc bead, through a copper bead, then through the opposite side of the disc bead.

8 Leave a 1cm tail of wire and bend it around the edge of the disc, to secure.

9 Pass the other end of the wire through the hole in the top of the pendant.

10 Wind the wire around a prong of your round nosed pliers, to form a bail.

11 Use a Gizmo tool to coil a length of wire. Secure 50cm of wire to the handle of the thinnest mandrel.

12 Coil the remainder of the wire.

13 If you don't have a Gizmo tool, wind the wire around a prong of your round nosed pliers, to form a coil.

14 Cut off two small coils approximately 5mm in length. Pull the remainder apart slightly, in the centre of the coil. Cut 80cm of cord and pass through one half of the coil, through the bail, then through the other half of the coil.

15 Pass the cord ends through the second copper bead, crossing them over to form a triangle. Then add a small coil on each side.

Making up the design:

1 The sliding knot uses the same macramé weave as is often seen in a 'friendship' bracelet, but it can also be used as a secure knot to complete your design.

Cut a 20cm length of matching cord for the knot, and fold it in half. Cross the two necklace cords over each other and place the loop of the knotting cord underneath them.

2 Cross the two ends of the knotting cord over. Pass the bottom knotting thread through the loop and pull tightly to secure.

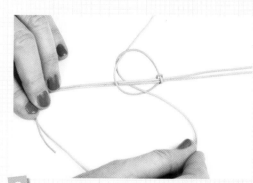

3 Place the necklace cords flat. You can pin them to your work surface to help secure them. This saves any confusion when knotting!

Lift the left knotting cord **over** the top of all the neck cords. Lift the right knotting cord **over** the cord you have just crossed over. Then thread it **under** the two neck cords and **through** the loop you have made on the left hand side. Pull to secure.

I say this to myself whenever I do a friendship/ square knot: **"Over, over, under and through!"**

4 Now repeat on the other side, so reversing your loop: lift the right knotting cord **over** the top of all neck cords. Lift the left knotting cord **over** the cord you have just crossed over. Then thread it **under** the two neck cords and **through** the loop on the right hand side. Pull to secure.

Repeat Steps 3 and 4, three times, to create your sliding knot.

5 Tie a knot in the two outside cords, as near as possible to the sliding knot. Then tie a knot at each end of the neck cords and paint with clear nail varnish or PVA glue to secure.

Here is a design using a square cutter and silver and black mottled Lisa Pavelka foils.

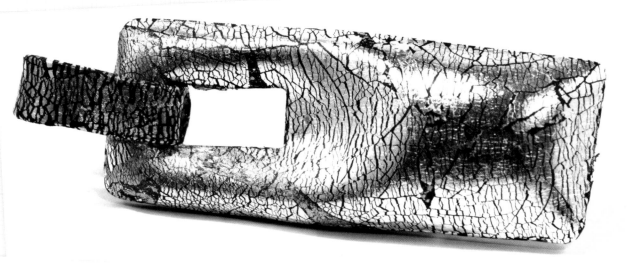

Hollow pendants can be made in so many different shapes.

Above: This rectangular design is made using a number '1' from a pack of number cookie cutters. Look around for various shapes and designs to give your range of jewellery the edge!

Left: To give your pendant a curved finish, bake on the side of a jam jar.

Opposite: This heart is made using the same technique but this time using a stunning combination of jewel shades.

Pass a sheet of clay though your clay roller, slice your leftover canes and place onto the clay. When you are happy with your design, either use an acrylic roller or put the clay through the roller again on the thickest setting before cutting your design.

Combine your polymer clay with gemstones to give an elegant, timeless look.

Sensational
Slices

Mokume Gane (Mo-koo-may Gar-ney)

I discovered this exciting technique whilst reading a book by Julie Picarello.

Layers and layers of clay colours, inks, and foils, make every piece of jewellery totally unique.

Whether you prefer an organic textured finish or the high shine of dichroic glass, Mokume Gane is for you!

Mokume Shield

A personal favourite, the design possibilities are endless.

Ingredients

- ☑ Polymer clay: one block of Translucent, half a block of Black

- ☑ One sheet of silver transfer foil, or silver leaf

- ☑ Jam jar

Instructions

1 Condition both clay colours. Roll each one through your clay roller on the thickest setting, usually number 1. Cut each of clays in half. Using your fingers, burnish silver transfer foil or small pieces of silver leaf onto one piece of Black and one piece of Translucent clay.

2 Cut the foiled Translucent clay in half. Cut the plain Translucent clay in half. Now stack your clays as follows: plain black, foiled Translucent, plain Translucent, foiled Black, plain Translucent then foiled Translucent.

3 Roll the stack through your clay roller on the thickest setting, usually number 1. Cut the stack in half and place the stacks on top of each other. Now the fun starts!!

4 Place the clay stack onto a tile. Make random indentations in the clay surface to produce patterns. You could use a knitting needle, clay cutter, cocktail stick, or any small object that will make a distinctive mark. As you push into the clay, the foil layers move randomly through the stack.

5 Bending a flexible clay cutting blade towards you in a slight curve, carefully cut your first slice.

6 Repeat to cut several thin slices from the stack. If you wish, you can add more indentations as you slice. Stack the slices on top of each other.

7 Create a decorative edge using a corrugated edge blade bent into a slight curve.

8 Place the decorated clay onto a double layer of plain black clay. Cut out a shield shape of your choice using the flexible cutting blade.

9 Cut two eye pins in half and push into the top of the pendant ready to hang. Now bake according to the manufacturer's instructions.

10 Thread the leather cord through the two eye pin loops, add a bead to each cord then feed the cords through the two hole connector. Finally feed through the Haematite tubes.

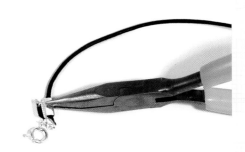

11 Place one end of the leather cord inside the cord ending. Using your flat nosed pliers fold over one side of the clasp. Now fold over the opposite side of the clasp to form a secure fastening.

12 Repeat on the other end of the leather cord.

Tile and Chain Bracelet

These Polymer Clay tiles give a new dimension
to the Chain Maille connections, perfect.

Ingredients

- ☑ Polymer clay: one block of Turquoise, half a block each of Burnt Umber, Rhino Grey and Translucent

- ☑ One sheet of silver transfer foil, or silver leaf

- ☑ Approximately 200 jump rings, 5mm external diameter

- ☑ Triple bar clasp with chain

- ☑ Metal ruler

Instructions

1 Condition all of the clay colours. Roll each one through your clay roller on the thickest setting, usually number 1. Cut the Turquoise clay in half and keep to one side for the tile backings. Using your fingers, burnish silver transfer foil or small pieces of silver leaf onto the Burnt Umber clay.

2 Stack your clays as follows: foiled Burnt Umber, Turquoise, Translucent, Rhino Grey, then Translucent. Roll the stack through your pasta roller on the thickest setting, usually number 1. Cut the stack into three pieces then place them on top of each other.

3 Place the clay stack onto a tile. Make random indentations in the clay surface using a cocktail stick or small cutters, to produce delicate patterns. As you push into the clay, the foil layers move randomly through the stack.

4 Next, cut a backing strip 10cm x 3cm from the leftover Turquoise clay. Bending a flexible clay cutting blade towards you in a slight curve, carefully cut enough thin slices from the stack to cover the backing strip. Lightly press them into the clay using an acrylic rolling sheet.

5 Using a metal ruler and your clay cutting blade, cut six clay tiles measuring 1.5cm x 2cm. Make three holes on each side of each tile, large enough for your jump rings to pass through. Bake the clay tiles according to the manufacturer's instructions.

Half Byzantine Weave: Chain Maille Connector Links

Polymer clay blends well with gemstones and chain, so this Chain Maille technique for joining two components together is not only useful, but adds extra glamour to your designs.

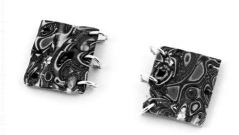

1 Open 180 jump rings. Place an open jump ring into every hole on both sides of each tile and close each ring.

2 Add two open rings onto each closed ring. Close those rings. Holding the closed rings together, thread two open jump rings onto them. Close the rings. Again, holding the closed rings together, thread two open jump rings onto them. Close the rings. You now have three sets of two jump rings.

3 Hold the first two rings together and allow the third set to fall open on each side.

4 Push apart the second set of rings then, using a cocktail stick, pull up the set of rings that fell apart in step 3.

5 Remove the cocktail stick, pick up an open jump ring and thread through the rings you have just folded back.

6 Repeat with a second jump ring. Through these rings thread on one open jump ring and pass it through the equivalent top hole on the left hand side of the next tile. Each set is made in the same way.

7 Repeat the Half Byzantine Weave between each tile until your bracelet has six tiles with three chain maille connector links between each one, plus three chain maille connector links at each end of the bracelet.

8 Attach a triple bar clasp to finish your bracelet design.

More Ideas

Far Right: This design is made in the same way as the previous design, but the tiles are threaded onto jewellery elastic. You may need eight or nine tiles depending on the size of your wrist. Cut the clay into 1.5cm x 2cm tiles. Using a pin or a cocktail stick, make two holes from side to side through each tile, between the decorated and backing layers. Ensure the holes are large enough to pass beading elastic through. Bake the tiles according to the manufacturer's instructions. Thread tiles and beads alternately onto jewellery elastic and secure the ends with jewellery glue or a drop of clear nail varnish.

Right: To make these pendants; use only Translucent clay and add alcohol inks to the surface of the silver transfer foil.

Little Stick of Rock!

Building a Cane

The term 'cane' comes from the world of glassmaking.

At the end of their working day, Italian glassblowers had many colourful glass rods left over from their work. The men stretched these rods very thinly and clustered them into long canes, then sliced the canes into clear glass domes to create the familiar paperweights that are still sold today.

The colourful glass slices looked like tiny flowers, hence the name Millefiori, Mille Fleur, or 'a thousand flowers'.

Millefiori is also associated with floral beads, but refers to any cane with a design that runs through it from one end to the other, similar to a stick of rock.

Bezel
Bracelet

The simplicity of this bracelet would work with
casual jeans or a night out to remember.

Ingredients

- ☑ Polymer Clay: Half a block each of White, Black and Silver
- ☑ Seven 8mm Bracelet bezel blanks
- ☑ Five 8mm gemstone beads of your choice
- ☑ One 6mm gemstone of your choice as a charm

Instructions

1 Condition all of the clay colours. Roll each one through your clay roller on the thickest setting, usually number 1. Roll the white clay into a 1.5cm diameter tube. Cut a strip of black clay and roll it around the white clay tube.

2 Slice off a quarter of the tube. Roll it to reduce it to half the original diameter. Slice it into four equal lengths and press the four lengths together to use as the centre stamen of the flower.

3 Add two more clay layers to the remaining tube. Cut a strip of silver clay and roll it around the tube. Then cut a strip of black clay and roll that around the tube.

4 Place the tube onto a cutting tile and slice it lengthwise down the centre, but don't cut right through. Open out the split tube as shown.

5 Roll a small amount of black clay through your the roller on a medium setting, usually 4 or 5. Cut a 1cm wide strip the same length as the tube, and place inside the split tube and close. This will give detail to each petal of the the flower. Trim the excess.

6 Now roll the tube, making sure not to twist it as you reduce it in size to 8mm wide. Cut into five petals. Pinch along the tube of clay where you inserted the strip in Step 5 to form a petal shaped cane.

7 Position the petals around the stamen to form a flower, making sure the centre of the petal touches the stamen from one end of the cane to the other.

8 Roll to reduce the large flower cane, until it is the correct diameter for the bracelet bezels.

9 Cut a slice of the large flower cane for each bezel. Press the slices into the bezels and carefully draw the blade over the surface of the bezel to take off the excess clay. Bake all of the clay filled bezels according to the manufacturer's instructions. Apply several layers of water-based varnish, allowing each layer to dry before applying the next to give a glossy finish.

10 Thread a gemstone onto an eye pin and trim the excess to 1cm. Using your round nosed pliers, hold the end of the eye pin and turn to form a loop. Repeat for all of the 8mm gemstones.

11 Hold one of the 8mm gemstones, open a loop on one side and feed on a bezel and close the loop. Link your design together, alternating gemstones and clay filled bezels to achieve the desired bracelet length. For the final gemstone charm you need to use a head pin so you will only need to make one loop to attach this to your design.

12 The bracelet in the picture has a final length of 7½ inches, you will see I then added a jump ring on one end and a jump ring and clasp to the other, but I had one bezel left over so I added this along with the charm as a feature.

Multi Cane Pendant

Combine your Polymer Clay canes to create a
truly unique pendant, make the design your own.

Ingredients

- ☑ Polymer Clay: one block of Black, half a block each of Ecru and Rhino Grey; a quarter block of White

- ☑ Scrap clay for inside the pendant (optional)

- ☑ One eye pin or a pendant bail

- ☑ Cling film

Instructions

Making Bulls Eye Canes

Making a Spiral Cane

Place the remaining sheet of Rhino Grey on top of the remaining sheet of Ecru and roll to form a spiral. Stop just before the final turn, and neaten the edge with a tissue blade. Roll the spiral cane to the same thickness as the bulls eye canes. Cut the spiral cane in half.

Condition your clay colours. Roll each of them through your clay roller on the thickest setting, usually number 1. Cut the black sheet into four. Cut the Ecru and Rhino Grey in half. Roll one piece of Ecru into a tube and cover with the square of White and a square of Black. Roll one piece of black into a tube and cover with Rhino Grey and Black. Keep the remaining black square for the back of the pendant.

Here is an alternative colour way for your pendant.

Use the same techniques, but add more colours to your canes.

Creating the pendant

1 Gently press all of the cane pieces to form oval shapes. Put a spiral cane on top of each bulls eye cane. Cut the canes in half and press together as shown.

2 Using your leftover or scrap clay, mould it into a triangle about 4cm in size. Gently smooth the corners with your fingers to make them more rounded. You can either leave the back as scrap clay if the colours co-ordinate with your design, or you can use the remaining sheet of black clay and press it carefully onto the back of your pendant to avoid air bubbles.

3 Using your tissue blade cut thin slices of your canes and add to your pendant as shown. Use your acrylic roller to gently roll over the surface to remove the joins.

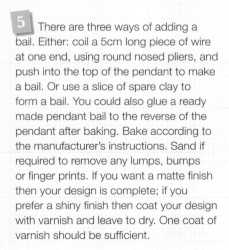

5 There are three ways of adding a bail. Either: coil a 5cm long piece of wire at one end, using round nosed pliers, and push into the top of the pendant to make a bail. Or use a slice of spare clay to form a bail. You could also glue a ready made pendant bail to the reverse of the pendant after baking. Bake according to the manufacturer's instructions. Sand if required to remove any lumps, bumps or finger prints. If you want a matte finish then your design is complete; if you prefer a shiny finish then coat your design with varnish and leave to dry. One coat of varnish should be sufficient.

4 Place a piece of cling film tightly over the pendant and rub firmly to smooth the surface. Remove the cling film.

Wire Bangle

A simple design that works well as a single bangle or worn as a multi layered cuff.

Ingredients

- ☑ Polymer Clay: thin scraps of Black, Pearl and Bronze
- ☑ 1.5m of 0.8mm gauge Copper wire
- ☑ Gizmo Wire Coiling Tool

Instructions

1 Cut your Pearl clay in half and roll one half into a tube. Now form two bulls eye canes: roll a strip of Black clay around the tube of Pearl clay. Repeat with a tiny strip of Pearl clay around a small tube of Bronze clay.

2 Use a long acrylic sheet to roll and lengthen the Black/Pearl bulls eye cane. Slice the Black/Pearl cane into five equal length tubes. Cut the Pearl/Bronze cane to the same length as one of the Black/White canes; this will be used as the centre of your design.

3 Arrange the five Black/Pearl bulls eye canes around the Pearl/Bronze bulls eye cane centre, to form a stylised flower cane.

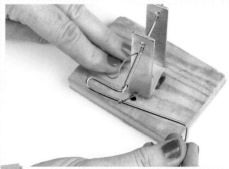

4 Use a Gizmo tool to coil a length of wire. Secure 50cm of wire to the handle of the thinnest mandrel.

5 Turn the handle to form a coil. Wrap the wire as far as you can along the mandrel, leaving a 5cm tail of wire at one end. Remove the coil. Repeat to make an identical length coil, but with a 10cm wire tail on one end.

6 Using the coil with the 10cm tail, secure the first 5cm to the handle of the thinnest mandrel on the Gizmo tool. Turn the handle and coil the remaining 5cm of wire then 'coil the coil' and when you reach the 5cm tail at the other end, make another small coil to secure.

7 Cut a separate length of wire that will fit around your wrist comfortably, adding 10cm for the loop clasp and spiral. Use flat nosed pliers to bend the wire approximately 5cm from one end.

8 I have found it easier to fit a polymer clay clasp through a triangular 'loop' clasp, rather than an oval shape. To form the triangle clasp, make a second bend 1cm away from the first.

9 Next wrap the short end around the wire to form a triangular loop. The size and shape of your clasp will depend on the polymer clay toggle bead that you create. I suggest making each side of your triangle 1cm in length.

10 Thread the 'coiled coil' and then the single wire coil onto bangle wire with the triangular loop clasp. Try the bangle around your wrist and shorten the single coil if necessary.

11 Now you have a bangle of coiled wire with a triangular loop clasp on one end. Trim excess wire at the other end to 4cm. Use round nosed pliers to form a loop on the end of the 4cm of wire; change to flat nosed pliers and spiral the remainder until you are 1cm from the end of the coiled bracelet. This doesn't need to be perfect because this spiral will be covered with clay. Place your flat nosed pliers against the end of your coil and bend the wire to form a hook. Check to make sure it will easily fit through the triangular loop clasp on the other end of the bangle.

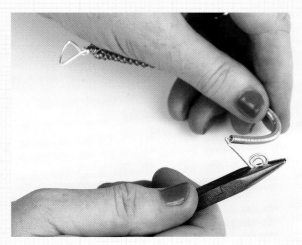

12 Cut a slice of flower cane approximately 5mm thick. Hold the slice then, using a tissue blade very carefully, make a cut half way through the slice of flower cane.

13 Push the spiral at the end of the bracelet into the slice of flower cane and press either side to secure the clay to the wire.

14 Smooth the clay and remember to try the clay bead through the triangular loop clasp before baking the clay onto the wire bangle. Then bake the bangle according to the manufacturer's instructions.

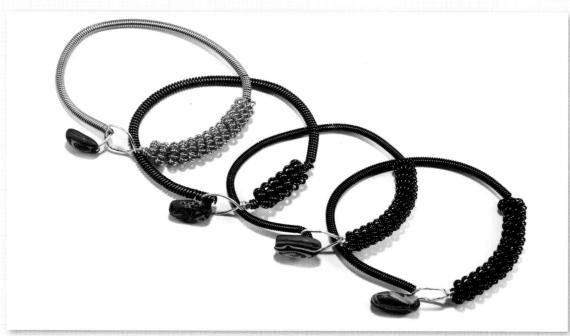

Your canes can be used in so many different ways.

To make this pendant, slice your canes and place onto a sheet of clay.

Use an acrylic roller or your clay roller to smooth the slices of canes into the sheet of clay.

Cut your design and bake on the side of a jam jar to give a beautiful curved finish.

The way you finish your design can make such a difference. Push a metal tube into your clay, remove to bake then glue in place when you have sanded and buffed your finished piece.

Take two slices of your cane and add black Onyx round beads to complete your earring design.

Tassel Necklace & Earrings

The combination of Pyrite and Amazonite work so well together, with a tassel of fresh spring like shades of Polymer Clay.

Ingredients

- ☑ Polymer clay: one block of Translucent, half a block each of Turquoise and Burnt Umber, a quarter block each of Peacock Pearl, Ecru

- ☑ Scrap clay for inside the leaf bud (optional)

- ☑ Approximately 80 mixed sizes of Pyrite rounds

- ☑ Approximately 16 Amazonite 6mm rounds or rondelles

- ☑ One 14mm wooden cube bead

- ☑ One 2cm diameter hollow wooden disc

- ☑ Approximately 2cm of chain

Instructions

1 Condition your clay colours. Roll each of them through your clay roller on the thickest setting, usually number 1. To create the delicate clay shades, use the following colour mixes:

A = half a block of Translucent + a small ball of Turquoise (the size of pea)

B = a quarter block of Translucent + a quarter block of Burnt Umber

2 Roll each of the mixes together in your hands. Fold in half, twist and roll them together again to start the blending process. Pass each mix through your clay roller on the thickest setting, usually number 1, then pass them through again on a medium setting, number 5, to complete the mixing process.

Centre Leaf

1 Create a "Skinner blend" using your turquoise and translucent mix, and an eighth block of translucent. Pass each colour through your clay roller on the thickest setting. Cut into two triangles as shown and fit together to form a rectangle. Fold the clay rectangle and pass through your pasta roller on the thickest setting, number 1. Folding in the same direction each time, fold and pass through again on a medium setting, number 5, to complete the blend.

2 Roll the blend into a tube starting with the lightest shade. Stand the tube on its end and press to form a short, thick cane.

3 Pass the remaining Burnt Umber through your clay roller on setting 6 or 7. Slice the short thick cane across the centre and place one side onto the Burnt Umber clay. Trim the Burnt Umber clay to size and fit the two cane halves back together around it. Slice either side of the centre vein and repeat, slicing as many times as you can to form the leaf veins.

4 Once the veins are complete, place the leaf cane onto your work surface with the stripes lying horizontally. Hold your tissue blade vertically across the stripes and tilt it a few degrees to the left, cutting through the stripes at an angle.

5 Turn one side over to match the veins together in a leaf shape as shown. Surround the leaf cane with a thin sheet of Peacock Pearl.

Wooden Bead and Leaf Bud

Striped Edging

Surround the leaf cane with a thin sheet of Burnt Umber. Now add a striped edging as follows: pass the remaining Turquoise mix, Translucent, Burnt Umber and Peacock Pearl clays through your clay roller on the thickest setting. Lay them on top of each other to form a striped cane. Slice into strips and cover the outside of the leaf cane. Squeeze into a leaf or tear drop shape, remembering to check both ends to make sure the pattern is the same.

Cut eight slices of leaf cane and place four of them around the wooden cube. They will stick without glue. Take a small ball of scrap clay and place the remaining four leaf slices around it. Push an eye pin into the top of the bud. Reduce the size of some of the remaining leaf cane and slice off small leaves to add to the tassel. Make a small hole in the end of each leaf with a cocktail stick or pin. Bake according to the manufacturer's instructions.

Creating the Necklace

1 Thread an eye pin through the top hole of your wooden cube and form a loop on the other end. Join the bud to one loop, eye pin to eye pin. Thread an eye pin through the top hole of the wooden disc, thread on a crimp bead as a spacer, an Amazonite bead, another crimp bead, another Amazonite bead and one final crimp bead. Thread the eye pin out through the bottom hole of the wooden disc and form a loop at the end.

2 Attach the cube bead to one end of the chain and the wooden disc at the other end. Pass a head-pin through each of six Amazonite beads, trim to 1cm and form a loop at the end. Add jump rings to the small leaves and randomly add the leaves and Amazonite charms along the chain to form a tassel.

3 Cut 75cm of beading thread. Thread a crimp and a clasp onto one end. Take the end of the thread back through the crimp. Push the crimp up to the clasp, and squash the crimp firmly with flat nosed pliers. Trim excess beading thread close to the crimp.

4 Take the Pyrite and remaining Amazonite beads and thread half of them onto the beading thread. Thread on the wooden disc and then the other half of your Pyrite and Amazonite beads. Repeat Step 3 on the other end of the thread with a jump ring instead of a clasp, making sure the excess thread is pulled through the crimp. Use crimp covers to cover the crimps, if you wish.

Leaf Earrings

1 To make a matching set of earrings, take two slices form the leaf cane and make a small hole in the top of each leaf. Bake according to the manufacturers' instructions. Thread a jump ring through the hole in each leaf.

2 Thread beads to match your necklace design onto an eyepin. Trim the eyepin to 1cm and form a loop at the end. Connect the beads and a leaf to a shepherd hook finding to complete your design. Repeat for the second earring.

Jewellery Maker Designers

Jewellery Maker TV prides themselves on the quality of their gemstones, so it only seems right to include a selection of gemstone jewellery.

Sheila Davies
Resident Designer Jewellery Maker TV
Cherry Blossom Necklace
Sheila can turn her hand to many crafts, but jewellery making has been her passion for the past 5 years, as the mother-in-law of the owner (Steve Bennett) you could say it runs in the family!
www.jewellerymaker.com

Linda Brumwell
Resident Designer Jewellery Maker TV
Pearl Lace Necklace
Linda's shows are memorable for the fun, laughter, and of course her beautiful jewellery creations. Also a member of the Jewellery Maker family!
www.jewellerymaker.com

Rachel Norris
Guest Designer Jewellery Maker TV
Rachel is a Guest Designer at Jewellery Maker TV, and was judges favourite on BBC2's Paul Martin's 'Handmade Revolution' in October 2012 and has been an exhibitor at the V&A museum in London in 2012.
www.jewellerydesignbyrachel.com

Laura Binding
Guest Designer
Jewellery Maker TV
Cuff Bracelet
Laura runs her own jewellery business as well as freelance Jewellery Designing and Teaching.
www.youniqueyou.com

Gemma Crow
Guest Designer
Jewellery Maker TV
Bridal Bouquet
Gemma is an extremely talented jewellery designer, artist and teacher.
www.gemmacrow.co.uk

Natalia Coleman
Guest Designer Jewellery Maker TV
Silver Fox with accent of gold
Natalia is an International Art Clay instructor; visit her web
site to see how to explore your creativity.
www.silverclaycreations.co.uk

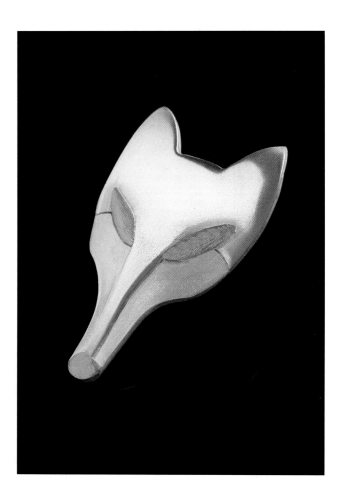

Hannah Oxberry
Product Manager Jewellery Maker TV
Butterfly Belle
Hannah is a qualified gemmologist and silversmith with 10
years experience in the jewellery trade.
www.anya-designs.co.uk
www.facebook.com/AnyaDesignsJewellery

Polymer Clay Designers

Debbie Carlton
Golden Leaf,
Cuff and Earring set
Debbie teaches introduction and advanced classes for precious metal clay and polymer clay from her studio in North West London.
www.debbiecarltonjewellery.co.uk
Debbie@debbiecarlton.com

Donna Kato
Monochrome Perfection Necklace
Donna Kato is a well-known international polymer clay artist and inspirational teacher. Her books are essential for anyone interested in the art of polymer clay.
www.katopolyclay.com
www.craftartedu.com

Alison Gallant
Beehive Necklace
As seen in Issue 17 of Making Jewellery magazine
Alison has 20 years experience of Polymer Clay design, her creations can be seen here in the UK in galleries and exhibitions.
www.millefioristudio.com

Bonnie McGough
Dragonfly
Bonnie is an artist, tutor, sculptor and writer who has been working in the field of polymer clay for many years.
www.bonniemcgough.com

Fiona Abel-Smith
Encased Evening Shades Necklace
Fiona is not only a Polymer Clay designer, but a very talented artist.
www.fionaabel-smith.co.uk

Birdy Heywood
Black and White Collection
Birdy has been a self confessed 'Polymer Clay Addict' for over 25 years.
www.birdyheywood.com

Index

Contacts & Websites

This book would not have been possible without the following suppliers of materials used within my projects, and the support of the following people:

Silver Clay Creations
www.silverclaycreations.co.uk
Natalia Coleman: it's because of this lovely lady that I took the plunge and put my projects to print.

Jewellery Maker TV
www.jewellerymaker.com
Eagle Road,
Moons Moat,
Redditch, B9 9HF
Telephone: 0800 6444 655
Supplier of all Gemstones, findings, PolymerClay, baking tray, clay roller, acrylic roller, blades, acrylic sheets, cutters, sanding pads, varnish, Lisa Pavelka foils and texture sheets, Mica Powder and the beading tool kit.

Birdy Heywood Polymer Clay Designs
www.birdyheywood.com
I blame Birdy for my addiction! I acknowledge her for her inspiration and creativity.

Chris Ham Photography
www.chrishamphotography.co.uk
Jewellery, product and sport photography. Thank you Chris for your patience and advice.

Sally Stevens
Email: sally.stevens@shiba.watrose.com
Writing services, editing, proofreading, indexing and business support services.

Julie Arnett
Email: julie.arnett@ymail.com
Typesetting, page layout, website and graphic design.

Lisa Pavelka
www.lisapavelka.com
Products to be used with Polymer and Metal Clays.